Singapore MATH

MENTAL MATH

Strategies and Process Skills to Develop Mental Calculation

Grade 2
(Level 1)

Thinking Kids®

An imprint of Carson-Dellosa Publishing LLC

Greensboro, North Carolina

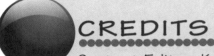

CREDITS

Content Editor: Karen Cermak-Serfass
Copy Editor: Barrie Hoople
Layout Design: Van Harris

This book has been correlated to state, common core state, national, and Canadian provincial standards. Visit carsondellosa.com to search for and view its correlations to your standards.

Copyright © 2011, Singapore Asia Publishers Pte Ltd

Thinking Kids®
An imprint of Carson-Dellosa Publishing LLC
PO Box 35665
Greensboro, NC 27425 USA

ISBN 978-1-936024-08-7

06-282171151

ABOUT THIS BOOK

Welcome to Singapore Math! The national math curriculum used in Singapore has been recognized worldwide for its excellence in producing students highly skilled in mathematics. The country's students have ranked at the top in achievement in the world on the Trends in International Mathematics and Science Study (TIMSS) in 1993, 1995, 2003, and 2008. The study also shows that students in Singapore are typically one grade level ahead of students in the United States. Because of these trends, Singapore Math has gained interest and popularity.

Mathematics in the Singapore primary (elementary) curriculum covers fewer topics but in greater depth. Key math concepts are introduced and built upon to reinforce various mathematical ideas and thinking. Singapore Math curriculum aims to help students develop the necessary math process skills for everyday life and to provide students with the opportunity to master math concepts.

Mental Math Level I, for grade 2, provides a comprehensive guide for mastering mental calculation. Each strategy in this book helps students perform mental calculation and obtain accurate answers in the shortest possible amount of time.

This book consists of 52 practice and review pages. Each practice page demonstrates a strategy with an example and includes 10 problems for students to solve. Students can then test their understanding by working on the review pages that are located after the practice pages.

To help students build and strengthen their mental calculation skills, this book provides strategies that will benefit students as they learn tips to solve math problems quickly and effectively. After acquiring such invaluable skills, students can apply them to their future, real-life experiences with math, such as in shopping and banking. *Mental Math Level I* is an indispensable resource for all students who wish to master mental strategies and excel in them.

TABLE OF CONTENTS

TABLE OF CONTENTS

STRATEGIES OVERVIEW

The following overview provides examples of the various math problem types and skill sets taught in Singapore Math.

1 Adding 0 to Numbers

$3 + 0 = 3$
- ☐ The sum of any number and 0 will always be the number.

2 Adding 1 to Numbers

$2 + 1 = 3$
- ☐ The sum of any number and 1 will always be one greater than the number.

3 Addition: Counting On from the First Number

$4 + 2 = 6$
- ☐ Count on from the first number the amount of the second number.

4 Addition: Counting On from the Larger Number

$2 + 5 = 7$
- ☐ Count on from the larger number the amount of the smaller number.

5 Adding Three Numbers

$1 + 3 + 2 = (1 + 3) + 2$
- ☐ Add the first two numbers.
$= 4 + 2$
- ☐ Add the third number to the sum to find the answer.
$= 6$

7 Adding 10 to Numbers

Numbers more than 10 can be read another way. The number 10 is known as 1 ten.

Examples: 11 = 1 ten 1 one
12 = 1 ten 2 ones
5 + 10 = 1 ten 5 ones
15

8 Adding Doubles

Adding doubles will result in an even number sum.
$1 + 1 = 2$
$2 + 2 = 4$
$3 + 3 = 6$
$4 + 4 = 8$
$5 + 5 = 10$

9 Addition: Breaking Up Numbers

$7 + 5 = 7 + 3 + 2$
- ☐ Break up the second number to make a ten.
$= (7 + 3) + 2$
$= 10 + 2$
- ☐ Add the numbers to find the answer.
$= 12$

10 Addition: Using Number Bonds (Part 1)

$28 + 5 = 20 + 8 + 5$
- ☐ Expand the two-digit number into tens and ones.
$= 20 + (8 + 2) + 3$
- ☐ Break up the one-digit number to make a ten.
$= 20 + 10 + 3$
- ☐ Add the numbers to find the answer.
$= 33$

11 Addition: Using Number Bonds (Part 2)

$17 + 18 = 10 + 7 + 10 + 8$
- ☐ Expand the numbers into tens and ones.
$= 10 + 10 + 7 + 8$
- ☐ Arrange the numbers to add the tens. Break up the last number to make a ten.
$= 20 + (7 + 3) + 5$
$= 20 + 10 + 5$
- ☐ Add the numbers to find the answer.
$= 35$

13 Addition: Using Number Bonds (Part 3)

$38 + 43 = 30 + 8 + 40 + 3$
- ☐ Expand the numbers into tens and ones.
$= 30 + 40 + 8 + 3$
- ☐ Arrange the numbers to add the tens values.
$= 70 + (8 + 2) + 1$
- ☐ Break up the last number to make a ten.
$= 70 + 10 + 1$
- ☐ Add the numbers to find the answer.
$= 81$

14 Addition: Rounding 9

$27 + 9$
$9 \approx 10$
- ☐ Round 9 up to the nearest ten.
$27 + 9 = 27 + (10 - 1)$
$= (27 + 10) - 1$
- ☐ Add the numbers.
$= 37 - 1$
- ☐ Since 1 was added to 9 to make 10, subtract 1 from the sum to find the answer.
$= 36$

15 Addition: Rounding 8

$24 + 8$
$8 \approx 10$
- ☐ Round 8 up to the nearest ten.
$24 + 8 = 24 + (10 - 2)$
$= (24 + 10) - 2$
- ☐ Add the numbers.
$= 34 - 2$
- ☐ Since 2 was added to 8 to make 10, subtract 2 from the sum to find the answer.
$= 32$

16 Addition: Rounding Numbers to Find Sums

$25 + 7$
$7 \approx 10$
- ☐ Round 7 up to the nearest ten.
$25 + 7 = 25 + (10 - 3)$
$= (25 + 10) - 3$
- ☐ Add the numbers.
$= 35 - 3$
- ☐ Since 3 was added to 7 to make 10, subtract 3 from the sum to find the answer.
$= 32$

Note: This strategy also works when adding numbers to 6. Subtract 4 when adding 10 to the number.

17 Addition: Using Fives

$26 + 7 = (25 + 1) + (5 + 2)$
- ☐ Break up each number into fives.
$= (25 + 5) + (2 + 1)$
- ☐ Arrange the numbers to add the fives.
$= 30 + 3$
- ☐ Add the numbers to find the answer.
$= 33$

19 Adding Tens

$58 + 20 = 50 + 8 + 20$
- ☐ Expand the first number into tens and ones.
$= 50 + 20 + 8$
- ☐ Arrange the numbers to add the tens values.
$= 70 + 8$
- ☐ Add the numbers to find the answer.
$= 78$

20 Subtracting 0 from Numbers

$19 - 0 = 19$
- ☐ The difference of any number and 0 will always be the number.

21 Subtracting 1 from Numbers

$34 - 1 = 33$
- ☐ The difference of any number and 1 will always be one less than the number.

22 Subtraction Facts: Counting Back (Part 1)

$5 - 2 = 3$
- ☐ Count back from the larger number the amount of the smaller number.

23 Subtraction Facts: Counting Back (Part 2)

$13 - 4 = 9$
- ☐ Count back from the larger number the amount of the smaller number.

25 Subtracting 10 from Numbers

Remember that numbers more than 10 can be read another way.

Examples: 15 = 1 ten 5 ones
16 = 1 ten 6 ones
17 = 1 ten 7 ones
18 = 1 ten 8 ones
19 = 1 ten 9 ones
20 = 1 ten 10 ones

$12 - 10 = 2$ ❑ Take away 1 ten and the answer will be the ones digit.

26 Subtracting Doubles

Knowing your doubles addition facts will help you subtract doubles.

$18 - 9 = 9$ $[9 + 9 = 18]$

Helpful Hint: When subtracting doubles, the answer will always be the smaller number.

27 Subtraction: Breaking Up Numbers

$23 - 5 = (13 + 10) - 5$ ❑ Break up the larger number into 10 and a number.

$= 13 + (10 - 5)$ ❑ Subtract the one-digit number from 10.

$= 13 + 5$ ❑ Add the numbers to find the answer.

$= 18$

28 Subtraction: Using Number Bonds (Part 1)

$14 - 2 = (10 + 4) - 2$ ❑ Expand the larger number into tens and ones.

$= 10 + (4 - 2)$ ❑ Subtract the one-digit numbers.

$= 10 + 2$ ❑ Add the numbers to find the answer.

$= 12$

29 Subtraction: Using Number Bonds (Part 2)

$22 - 5 = 22 - (2 + 3)$ ❑ Break up the one-digit number.

$= (22 - 2) - 3$ ❑ Make a tens value for easy subtraction.

$= 20 - 3$ ❑ Subtract the numbers to find the answer.

$= 17$

Helpful Hint: Use the ones digit from the minuend when you break up the one-digit number. In this problem, $22 - 5 = 22 - (2 + 3)$.

31 Subtraction: Using Number Bonds (Part 3)

$48 - 15 = (40 + 8) - (10 + 5)$ ❑ Expand the numbers into tens and ones.

$= (40 - 10) + (8 - 5)$ ❑ Arrange the numbers to subtract the tens and then the ones.

$= 30 + 3$ ❑ Add the numbers to find the answer.

$= 33$

32 Subtraction: Rounding 9

$38 - 9$

$9 \approx 10$ ❑ Round 9 up to the nearest 10.

$38 - 9 = 38 - 10 + 1$

$= (38 - 10) + 1$ ❑ Subtract the numbers.

$= 28 + 1$ ❑ Since 1 more than 9 was subtracted, add 1 to find the answer.

$= 29$

33 Subtraction: Rounding 8

$42 - 8$

$8 \approx 10$ ❑ Round 8 up to the nearest 10.

$42 - 8 = 42 - 10 + 2$

$= (42 - 10) + 2$ ❑ Subtract the numbers.

$= 32 + 2$ ❑ Since 2 more than 8 was subtracted, add 2 to find the answer.

$= 34$

34 Subtraction: Rounding 7

$51 - 7$

$7 \approx 10$ ❑ Round 7 up to the nearest 10.

$51 - 7 = 51 - 10 + 3$

$= (51 - 10) + 3$ ❑ Subtract the numbers.

$= 41 + 3$ ❑ Since 3 more than 7 was subtracted, add 3 to find the answer.

$= 44$

35 Subtracting Tens

$83 - 40 = (80 + 3) - 40$ ❑ Expand the first number into tens and ones.

$= (80 - 40) + 3$ ❑ Arrange the numbers to subtract the tens values.

$= 40 + 3$ ❑ Add the numbers to find the answer.

$= 43$

37 Multiplying Numbers by 0

$4 \times 0 = 0$ ❑ The product of any number times 0 will always be 0.

38 Multiplying Numbers by 1

$12 \times 1 = 12$ ❑ The product of any number times 1 will always be the number.

39 Multiplying Numbers by 2

$3 \times 2 = 3 + 3$ ❑ The product of any number times 2 is the same as adding doubles of that number.

$= 6$

40 Multiplying Numbers by 3

$4 \times 3 = (4 \times 2) + (4 \times 1)$ ❑ Break up the factor 3 into 2 and 1. Multiply the first factor by both 2 and 1.

$= 8 + 4$ ❑ Add the numbers to find the answer.

$= 12$

41 Multiplying Numbers by 4

$6 \times 4 = (6 \times 2) + (6 \times 2)$ ❑ Break up the factor 4 into 2 and 2. Multiply the first factor by 2 twice.

$= 12 + 12$ ❑ Add the doubles to find the answer.

$= 24$

43 Time: 1 Hour Before

What time is 1 hour before 3 o'clock?

$3 - 1 = 2$ ❑ The word *before* tells you to count back.

1 hour before 3 o'clock is **2 o'clock**

44 Time: 1 Hour After

What time is 1 hour after 3 o'clock?

$3 + 1 = 4$ ❑ The word *after* tells you to count on.

1 hour after 3 o'clock is **4 o'clock**

STRATEGY

Adding 0 to Numbers

Strategy

3 + 0 = **3**

❏ The sum of any number and 0 will always be the number.

Solve each problem mentally.

1. 6 + 0 =

2. 2 + 0 =

3. 0 + 10 =

4. 0 + 5 =

5. 0 + 1 =

6. 9 + 0 =

7. 7 + 0 =

8. 0 + 3 =

9. 8 + 0 =

10. 0 + 4 =

Adding 1 to Numbers

Strategy

2 + 1 = **3**

❏ The sum of any number and 1 will always be one greater than the number.

Solve each problem mentally.

1. 1 + 8 =

2. 0 + 1 =

3. 6 + 1 =

4. 1 + 1 =

5. 1 + 4 =

6. 7 + 1 =

7. 9 + 1 =

8. 1 + 2 =

9. 3 + 1 =

10. 1 + 5 =

Addition: Counting On from the First Number

Strategy

$4 + 2 = \mathbf{6}$

❑ Count on from the first number the amount of the second number.

Solve each problem mentally.

1. $5 + 2 =$
2. $8 + 1 =$
3. $7 + 3 =$
4. $6 + 2 =$
5. $4 + 1 =$
6. $9 + 1 =$
7. $3 + 2 =$
8. $4 + 3 =$
9. $7 + 2 =$
10. $4 + 4 =$

Addition: Counting On from the Larger Number

Strategy

$2 + 5 = 7$

❏ Count on from the larger number the amount of the smaller number.

Solve each problem mentally.

1. $2 + 3 =$

2. $7 + 2 =$

3. $3 + 6 =$

4. $4 + 2 =$

5. $2 + 6 =$

6. $3 + 5 =$

7. $3 + 7 =$

8. $2 + 8 =$

9. $5 + 2 =$

10. $4 + 5 =$

Adding Three Numbers

Strategy

$1 + 3 + 2 = (1 + 3) + 2$
$ = 4 + 2$
$ = \textbf{6}$

❑ Add the first two numbers.
❑ Add the third number to the sum to find the answer.

Solve each problem mentally.

1. $2 + 2 + 1 =$

2. $3 + 5 + 2 =$

3. $1 + 1 + 4 =$

4. $5 + 2 + 1 =$

5. $3 + 4 + 2 =$

6. $2 + 3 + 1 =$

7. $2 + 7 + 1 =$

8. $1 + 6 + 2 =$

9. $1 + 3 + 3 =$

10. $4 + 4 + 2 =$

GENERAL REVIEW 1

Solve each problem mentally.

1. 3 + 3 + 3 =

2. 5 + 0 =

3. 1 + 7 =

4. 2 + 4 + 1 =

5. 4 + 1 =

6. 3 + 4 =

7. 1 + 6 + 2 =

8. 4 + 6 =

9. 5 + 2 + 1 =

10. 2 + 2 + 6 =

Adding 10 to Numbers

Strategy

Numbers more than 10 can be read another way. The number 10 is known as 1 ten.

Examples: 11 = 1 ten 1 one
12 = 1 ten 2 ones

5 + 10 = 1 ten 5 ones
⎣→ 15

Solve each problem mentally.

1. 3 + 10 =

2. 10 + 0 =

3. 10 + 8 =

4. 2 + 10 =

5. 10 + 9 =

6. 10 + 1 =

7. 6 + 10 =

8. 10 + 7 =

9. 4 + 10 =

10. 10 + 10 =

STRATEGY

Adding Doubles

Strategy

Adding doubles will result in an even number sum.

$1 + 1 = 2$
$2 + 2 = 4$
$3 + 3 = 6$
$4 + 4 = 8$
$5 + 5 = 10$

Solve each problem mentally.

1. $10 + 10 =$

2. $3 + 3 =$

3. $4 + 4 =$

4. $2 + 2 =$

5. $6 + 6 =$

6. $7 + 7 =$

7. $5 + 5 =$

8. $9 + 9 =$

9. $20 + 20 =$

10. $11 + 11 =$

Addition: Breaking Up Numbers

Strategy

7 + 5 = 7 + 3 + 2
    = (7 + 3) + 2
    = 10 + 2
    = **12**

❑ Break up the second number to make a ten.
❑ Add the numbers to find the answer.

Solve each problem mentally.

1. 9 + 4 =

2. 7 + 6 =

3. 6 + 5 =

4. 5 + 8 =

5. 3 + 9 =

6. 5 + 9 =

7. 8 + 7 =

8. 3 + 8 =

9. 4 + 7 =

10. 9 + 6 =

STRATEGY

Addition: Using Number Bonds (Part 1)

Strategy

$28 + 5 = 20 + 8 + 5$ ❑ Expand the two-digit number into tens and ones.

$= 20 + (8 + 2) + 3$ ❑ Break up the one-digit number to make a ten.

$= 20 + 10 + 3$ ❑ Add the numbers to find the answer.

$= $ **33**

Solve each problem mentally.

1. $17 + 4 = $

2. $19 + 5 = $

3. $26 + 6 = $

4. $16 + 7 = $

5. $12 + 8 = $

6. $29 + 8 = $

7. $15 + 7 = $

8. $28 + 4 = $

9. $13 + 8 = $

10. $24 + 9 = $

STRATEGY

Addition: Using Number Bonds (Part 2)

Strategy

$17 + 18 = 10 + 7 + 10 + 8$ ❑ Expand the numbers into tens and ones.

$= 10 + 10 + 7 + 8$ ❑ Arrange the numbers to add the tens. Break up the last number to make a ten.

$= 20 + (7 + 3) + 5$

$= 20 + 10 + 5$ ❑ Add the numbers to find the answer.

$= \textbf{35}$

Solve each problem mentally.

1. $19 + 18 =$

2. $18 + 16 =$

3. $12 + 19 =$

4. $17 + 18 =$

5. $17 + 19 =$

6. $16 + 15 =$

7. $12 + 15 =$

8. $19 + 15 =$

9. $14 + 18 =$

10. $15 + 17 =$

GENERAL REVIEW 2

Solve each problem mentally.

1. 12 + 12 =

2. 9 + 5 =

3. 18 + 9 =

4. 18 + 17 =

5. 6 + 10 =

6. 4 + 10 =

7. 8 + 15 =

8. 8 + 6 =

9. 26 + 7 =

10. 22 + 22 =

Addition: Using Number Bonds (Part 3)

Strategy

$38 + 43 = 30 + 8 + 40 + 3$ ❏ Expand the numbers into tens and ones.

$= 30 + 40 + 8 + 3$ ❏ Arrange the numbers to add the tens values.

$= 70 + (8 + 2) + 1$ ❏ Break up the last number to make a ten.

$= 70 + 10 + 1$ ❏ Add the numbers to find the answer.

$= \mathbf{81}$

Solve each problem mentally.

1. $45 + 37 =$

2. $38 + 27 =$

3. $18 + 75 =$

4. $12 + 69 =$

5. $26 + 58 =$

6. $19 + 29 =$

7. $57 + 28 =$

8. $35 + 68 =$

9. $48 + 36 =$

10. $79 + 11 =$

STRATEGY

Addition: Rounding 9

Strategy

$27 + 9$
$9 \approx 10$
$27 + 9 = 27 + (10 - 1)$
$\quad = (27 + 10) - 1$
$\quad = 37 - 1$
$\quad = \mathbf{36}$

❑ Round 9 up to the nearest ten.

❑ Add the numbers.

❑ Since 1 was added to 9 to make 10, subtract 1 from the sum to find the answer.

Solve each problem mentally.

1. $18 + 9 =$

2. $36 + 9 =$

3. $88 + 9 =$

4. $49 + 9 =$

5. $22 + 9 =$

6. $67 + 9 =$

7. $53 + 9 =$

8. $44 + 9 =$

9. $78 + 9 =$

10. $56 + 9 =$

STRATEGY

Addition: Rounding 8

Strategy

24 + 8
8 ≈ 10
24 + 8 = 24 + (10 − 2)
     = (24 + 10) − 2
     = 34 − 2
     = **32**

❑ Round 8 up to the nearest ten.

❑ Add the numbers.

❑ Since 2 was added to 8 to make 10, subtract 2 from the sum to find the answer.

Solve each problem mentally.

1. 14 + 8 =
2. 36 + 8 =
3. 72 + 8 =
4. 53 + 8 =
5. 45 + 8 =
6. 66 + 8 =
7. 33 + 8 =
8. 78 + 8 =
9. 86 + 8 =
10. 59 + 8 =

Addition: Rounding Numbers to Find Sums

Strategy

25 + 7

7 ≈ 10   ❑ Round 7 up to the nearest ten.

25 + 7 = 25 + (10 − 3)

= (25 + 10) − 3   ❑ Add the numbers.

= 35 − 3   ❑ Since 3 was added to 7 to make 10,
subtract 3 from the sum to find the answer.

= **32**

Note: This strategy also works when adding numbers to 6. Subtract 4 when adding 10 to the number.

Solve each problem mentally.

1. 49 + 7 =

2. 35 + 7 =

3. 75 + 7 =

4. 56 + 7 =

5. 28 + 7 =

6. 88 + 7 =

7. 39 + 6 =

8. 64 + 6 =

9. 57 + 6 =

10. 78 + 6 =

Addition: Using Fives

Strategy

26 + 7 = (25 + 1) + (5 + 2)   ❑ Break up each number into fives.
     = (25 + 5) + (2 + 1)   ❑ Arrange the numbers to add the fives.
     = 30 + 3   ❑ Add the numbers to find the answer.
     = **33**

Solve each problem mentally.

1. 37 + 6 =

2. 58 + 9 =

3. 87 + 6 =

4. 46 + 6 =

5. 39 + 8 =

6. 58 + 7 =

7. 28 + 9 =

8. 76 + 6 =

9. 67 + 5 =

10. 19 + 9 =

GENERAL REVIEW 3

Solve each problem mentally.

1. 86 + 7 =

2. 13 + 9 =

3. 62 + 19 =

4. 45 + 7 =

5. 77 + 8 =

6. 35 + 39 =

7. 16 + 15 =

8. 58 + 6 =

9. 28 + 8 =

10. 19 + 18 =

25

STRATEGY

Adding Tens

Strategy

58 + 20 = 50 + 8 + 20
    = 50 + 20 + 8
    = 70 + 8
    = **78**

❑ Expand the first number into tens and ones.
❑ Arrange the numbers to add the tens values.
❑ Add the numbers to find the answer.

Solve each problem mentally.

1. 44 + 50 =

2. 78 + 10 =

3. 29 + 60 =

4. 55 + 30 =

5. 18 + 70 =

6. 63 + 30 =

7. 32 + 40 =

8. 41 + 30 =

9. 11 + 80 =

10. 73 + 20 =

STRATEGY

Subtracting 0 from Numbers

Strategy

$19 - 0 = \textbf{19}$

❑ The difference of any number and 0 will always be the number.

Solve each problem mentally.

1. $8 - 0 =$

2. $4 - 0 =$

3. $9 - 0 =$

4. $2 - 0 =$

5. $32 - 0 =$

6. $67 - 0 =$

7. $43 - 0 =$

8. $16 - 0 =$

9. $29 - 0 =$

10. $57 - 0 =$

STRATEGY

Subtracting 1 from Numbers

Strategy

34 – 1 = **33**

❑ The difference of any number and 1 will always be one less than the number.

Solve each problem mentally.

1. 5 – 1 =

2. 3 – 1 =

3. 9 – 1 =

4. 12 – 1 =

5. 38 – 1 =

6. 47 – 1 =

7. 86 – 1 =

8. 53 – 1 =

9. 29 – 1 =

10. 98 – 1 =

STRATEGY

Subtraction Facts: Counting Back (Part 1)

Strategy

5 – 2 = **3**

❑ Count back from the larger number the amount of the smaller number.

Solve each problem mentally.

1. 9 – 4 =

2. 8 – 7 =

3. 7 – 3 =

4. 5 – 1 =

5. 6 – 3 =

6. 9 – 2 =

7. 8 – 5 =

8. 6 – 2 =

9. 7 – 6 =

10. 8 – 4 =

Subtraction Facts: Counting Back (Part 2)

Strategy

13 – 4 = **9**

❑ Count back from the larger number the amount of the smaller number.

Solve each problem mentally.

I. 18 – 6 =

2. 25 – 4 =

3. 50 – 3 =

4. 19 – 5 =

5. 36 – 4 =

6. 99 – 6 =

7. 58 – 2 =

8. 70 – 7 =

9. 85 – 5 =

10. 67 – 6 =

GENERAL REVIEW 4

Solve each problem mentally.

1. 59 – 0 =

2. 36 + 60 =

3. 26 – 5 =

4. 7 – 6 =

5. 9 – 5 =

6. 18 + 40 =

7. 47 – 1 =

8. 79 – 5 =

9. 60 – 8 =

10. 78 + 20 =

STRATEGY

Subtracting 10 from Numbers

Strategy

Remember that numbers more than 10 can be read another way.

Examples: 15 = 1 ten 5 ones
16 = 1 ten 6 ones
17 = 1 ten 7 ones
18 = 1 ten 8 ones
19 = 1 ten 9 ones
20 = 1 ten 10 ones

$12 - 10 = \mathbf{2}$ ❑ Take away 1 ten and the answer will be the ones digit.

Solve each problem mentally.

1. 16 – 10 =

2. 11 – 10 =

3. 15 – 10 =

4. 10 – 10 =

5. 17 – 10 =

6. 13 – 10 =

7. 18 – 10 =

8. 14 – 10 =

9. 19 – 10 =

10. 20 – 10 =

Subtracting Doubles

Strategy

Knowing your doubles addition facts will help you subtract doubles.

18 − 9 = **9**   [9 + 9 = 18]

Helpful Hint: When subtracting doubles, the answer will always be the smaller number.

Solve each problem mentally.

1. 16 − 8 =

2. 26 − 13 =

3. 40 − 20 =

4. 12 − 6 =

5. 28 − 14 =

6. 22 − 11 =

7. 14 − 7 =

8. 30 − 15 =

9. 34 − 17 =

10. 10 − 5 =

Subtraction: Breaking Up Numbers

Strategy

$23 - 5 = (13 + 10) - 5$ ❑ Break up the larger number into 10 and a number.

$\quad\quad = 13 + (10 - 5)$ ❑ Subtract the one-digit number from 10.

$\quad\quad = 13 + 5$ ❑ Add the numbers to find the answer.

$\quad\quad = \mathbf{18}$

Solve each problem mentally.

1. $13 - 9 =$

2. $25 - 7 =$

3. $32 - 5 =$

4. $81 - 4 =$

5. $43 - 7 =$

6. $62 - 5 =$

7. $22 - 6 =$

8. $73 - 4 =$

9. $64 - 5 =$

10. $93 - 7 =$

Subtraction: Using Number Bonds (Part 1)

Strategy

$14 - 2 = (10 + 4) - 2$ ❑ Expand the larger number into tens and ones.

$= 10 + (4 - 2)$ ❑ Subtract the one-digit numbers.

$= 10 + 2$ ❑ Add the numbers to find the answer.

$= \mathbf{12}$

Solve each problem mentally.

1. $15 - 3 =$

2. $19 - 6 =$

3. $17 - 7 =$

4. $15 - 4 =$

5. $18 - 5 =$

6. $19 - 8 =$

7. $19 - 3 =$

8. $19 - 5 =$

9. $17 - 4 =$

10. $18 - 7 =$

Subtraction: Using Number Bonds (Part 2)

Strategy

$22 - 5 = 22 - (2 + 3)$
$ = (22 - 2) - 3$
$ = 20 - 3$
$ = \textbf{17}$

❏ Break up the one-digit number.
❏ Make a tens value for easy subtraction.
❏ Subtract the numbers to find the answer.

Helpful Hint: Use the ones digit from the minuend when you break up the one-digit number. In this problem, $22 - 5 = 2\textbf{2} - (\textbf{2} + 3)$.

Solve each problem mentally.

1. $25 - 9 =$

2. $36 - 8 =$

3. $33 - 4 =$

4. $23 - 7 =$

5. $16 - 9 =$

6. $22 - 7 =$

7. $35 - 6 =$

8. $15 - 8 =$

9. $21 - 9 =$

10. $14 - 8 =$

GENERAL REVIEW 5

Solve each problem mentally.

1. 34 − 7 =

2. 18 − 10 =

3. 32 − 16 =

4. 24 − 7 =

5. 32 − 5 =

6. 40 − 8 =

7. 14 − 10 =

8. 16 − 7 =

9. 38 − 4 =

10. 42 − 21 =

Subtraction: Using Number Bonds (Part 3)

Strategy

$48 - 15 = (40 + 8) - (10 + 5)$ ❏ Expand the numbers into tens and ones.

$= (40 - 10) + (8 - 5)$ ❏ Arrange the numbers to subtract the tens and then the ones.

$= 30 + 3$ ❏ Add the numbers to find the answer.

$= \mathbf{33}$

Solve each problem mentally.

1. $85 - 13 =$

2. $67 - 12 =$

3. $39 - 15 =$

4. $54 - 11 =$

5. $47 - 16 =$

6. $99 - 38 =$

7. $27 - 12 =$

8. $86 - 42 =$

9. $59 - 16 =$

10. $74 - 12 =$

STRATEGY

Subtraction: Rounding 9

Strategy

$38 - 9$

$9 \approx 10$ ❏ Round 9 up to the nearest 10.

$38 - 9 = 38 - 10 + 1$

         $= (38 - 10) + 1$ ❏ Subtract the numbers.

         $= 28 + 1$ ❏ Since 1 more than 9 was subtracted, add 1

         $= \mathbf{29}$ to find the answer.

Solve each problem mentally.

1. $57 - 9 =$

2. $36 - 9 =$

3. $65 - 9 =$

4. $44 - 9 =$

5. $25 - 9 =$

6. $71 - 9 =$

7. $85 - 9 =$

8. $90 - 9 =$

9. $53 - 9 =$

10. $82 - 9 =$

STRATEGY

Subtraction: Rounding 8

Strategy

$42 - 8$
$8 \approx 10$
$42 - 8 = 42 - 10 + 2$
$\qquad = (42 - 10) + 2$
$\qquad = 32 + 2$
$\qquad = \textbf{34}$

❑ Round 8 up to the nearest 10.

❑ Subtract the numbers.
❑ Since 2 more than 8 was subtracted, add 2 to find the answer.

Solve each problem mentally.

1. $91 - 8 =$

2. $50 - 8 =$

3. $63 - 8 =$

4. $45 - 8 =$

5. $82 - 8 =$

6. $67 - 8 =$

7. $34 - 8 =$

8. $15 - 8 =$

9. $93 - 8 =$

10. $26 - 8 =$

STRATEGY

Subtraction: Rounding 7

Strategy

51 – 7

7 ≈ 10 ❑ Round 7 up to the nearest 10.

51 – 7 = 51 – 10 + 3

= (51 – 10) + 3 ❑ Subtract the numbers.

= 41 + 3 ❑ Since 3 more than 7 was subtracted, add 3

= **44** to find the answer.

Solve each problem mentally.

1. 23 – 7 =

2. 45 – 7 =

3. 93 – 7 =

4. 72 – 7 =

5. 16 – 7 =

6. 32 – 7 =

7. 56 – 7 =

8. 63 – 7 =

9. 96 – 7 =

10. 84 – 7 =

STRATEGY

Subtracting Tens

Strategy

83 – 40 = (80 + 3) – 40	❑ Expand the first number into tens and ones.
= (80 – 40) + 3	❑ Arrange the numbers to subtract the tens values.
= 40 + 3	❑ Add the numbers to find the answer.
= **43**	

Solve each problem mentally.

1. 45 – 20 =

2. 51 – 40 =

3. 96 – 30 =

4. 29 – 10 =

5. 73 – 50 =

6. 64 – 30 =

7. 38 – 20 =

8. 79 – 40 =

9. 99 – 60 =

10. 87 – 70 =

GENERAL REVIEW 6

Solve each problem mentally.

1. $72 - 11 =$

2. $21 - 8 =$

3. $37 - 9 =$

4. $63 - 7 =$

5. $95 - 13 =$

6. $52 - 7 =$

7. $81 - 50 =$

8. $49 - 9 =$

9. $73 - 40 =$

10. $43 - 8 =$

Multiplying Numbers by 0

Strategy

4 × 0 = **0**

❏ The product of any number times 0 will always be 0.

Solve each problem mentally.

1. 8 × 0 =

2. 2 × 0 =

3. 5 × 0 =

4. 9 × 0 =

5. 6 × 0 =

6. 3 × 0 =

7. 10 × 0 =

8. 7 × 0 =

9. 11 × 0 =

10. 1 × 0 =

STRATEGY

Multiplying Numbers by 1

Strategy

12 × 1 = **12**

❏ The product of any number times 1 will always be the number.

Solve each problem mentally.

1. 2 × 1 =

2. 6 × 1 =

3. 5 × 1 =

4. 10 × 1 =

5. 7 × 1 =

6. 3 × 1 =

7. 1 × 1 =

8. 9 × 1 =

9. 8 × 1 =

10. 11 × 1 =

STRATEGY

Multiplying Numbers by 2

Strategy

$3 \times 2 = 3 + 3$
     $= 6$

❏ The product of any number times 2 is the same as adding doubles of that number.

Solve each problem mentally.

1. $4 \times 2 =$

2. $10 \times 2 =$

3. $8 \times 2 =$

4. $5 \times 2 =$

5. $1 \times 2 =$

6. $6 \times 2 =$

7. $2 \times 2 =$

8. $7 \times 2 =$

9. $9 \times 2 =$

10. $12 \times 2 =$

STRATEGY

Multiplying Numbers by 3

Strategy

$4 \times 3 = (4 \times 2) + (4 \times 1)$ ❑ Break up the factor 3 into 2 and 1. Multiply the first factor by both 2 and 1.

$= 8 + 4$ ❑ Add the numbers to find the answer.

$= \mathbf{12}$

Solve each problem mentally.

1. $3 \times 3 =$

2. $6 \times 3 =$

3. $9 \times 3 =$

4. $5 \times 3 =$

5. $1 \times 3 =$

6. $2 \times 3 =$

7. $7 \times 3 =$

8. $12 \times 3 =$

9. $10 \times 3 =$

10. $8 \times 3 =$

STRATEGY

Multiplying Numbers by 4

Strategy

$6 \times 4 = (6 \times 2) + (6 \times 2)$ ❑ Break up the factor 4 into 2 and 2. Multiply the first factor by 2 twice.

$= 12 + 12$ ❑ Add the doubles to find the answer.

$= \textbf{24}$

Solve each problem mentally.

1. $7 \times 4 =$

2. $10 \times 4 =$

3. $12 \times 4 =$

4. $3 \times 4 =$

5. $2 \times 4 =$

6. $5 \times 4 =$

7. $8 \times 4 =$

8. $9 \times 4 =$

9. $4 \times 4 =$

10. $1 \times 4 =$

GENERAL REVIEW 7

Solve each problem mentally.

1. 3 × 2 =

2. 8 × 0 =

3. 5 × 1 =

4. 2 × 4 =

5. 6 × 4 =

6. 9 × 2 =

7. 10 × 3 =

8. 12 × 0 =

9. 1 × 1 =

10. 7 × 3 =

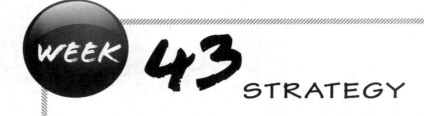

STRATEGY

Time: 1 Hour Before

Strategy

What time is 1 hour before 3 o'clock?

3 − 1 = 2   ❑ The word *before* tells you to count back.

1 hour before 3 o'clock is **2 o'clock**

Find each time mentally.

1. What time is 1 hour before 12 o'clock?

2. What time is 1 hour before 6 o'clock?

3. What time is 1 hour before 2 o'clock?

4. What time is 1 hour before 8 o'clock?

5. What time is 1 hour before 4 o'clock?

6. What time is 1 hour before 7 o'clock?

7. What time is 1 hour before 5 o'clock?

8. What time is 1 hour before 9 o'clock?

9. What time is 1 hour before 10 o'clock?

10. What time is 1 hour before 11 o'clock?

STRATEGY

Time: 1 Hour After

Strategy

What time is 1 hour after 3 o'clock?

$3 + 1 = 4$ ❑ The word *after* tells you to count on.

1 hour after 3 o'clock is **4 o'clock**

Find each time mentally.

1. What time is 1 hour after 6 o'clock?

2. What time is 1 hour after 8 o'clock?

3. What time is 1 hour after 11 o'clock?

4. What time is 1 hour after 2 o'clock?

5. What time is 1 hour after 9 o'clock?

6. What time is 1 hour after 7 o'clock?

7. What time is 1 hour after 1 o'clock?

8. What time is 1 hour after 5 o'clock?

9. What time is 1 hour after 10 o'clock?

10. What time is 1 hour after 4 o'clock?

GENERAL REVIEW 8

Solve each problem mentally.

1. 8 + 4 =

2. 14 + 0 =

3. 3 + 2 + 4 =

4. 35 − 4 =

5. 38 − 19 =

6. 3 × 4 =

7. 17 + 30 =

8. 46 − 10 =

9. 8 × 2 =

10. 17 + 17 =

GENERAL REVIEW 9

Solve each problem mentally.

1. 48 + 9 =

2. 50 − 0 =

3. 6 × 3 =

4. 29 − 13 =

5. 98 − 40 =

6. 39 + 10 =

7. 63 + 6 =

8. 16 + 28 =

9. 21 − 8 =

10. 8 × 0 =

WEEK 47

GENERAL REVIEW 10

Solve each problem mentally.

1. 29 – 10 =

2. 62 + 9 =

3. 7 + 1 =

4. 35 + 17 =

5. 56 – 19 =

6. 89 – 1 =

7. 10 × 1 =

8. 48 – 9 =

9. What time is 1 hour before 11 o'clock?

10. 85 + 12 =

GENERAL REVIEW 11

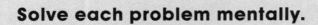

Solve each problem mentally.

1. $9 \times 4 =$

2. $38 + 45 =$

3. $16 - 3 =$

4. $9 + 9 =$

5. $56 + 0 =$

6. $23 + 9 =$

7. $42 - 7 =$

8. $37 + 26 =$

9. $6 \times 2 =$

10. $91 - 50 =$

GENERAL REVIEW 12

Solve each problem mentally.

1. $89 - 6 =$

2. $14 - 7 =$

3. What time is 1 hour after 9 o'clock?

4. $3 \times 6 =$

5. $27 + 15 =$

6. $83 + 10 =$

7. What time is 1 hour before 6 o'clock?

8. $31 - 7 =$

9. $42 + 8 =$

10. $75 + 6 =$

WEEK 50

GENERAL REVIEW 13

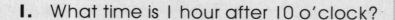

Solve each problem mentally.

1. What time is 1 hour after 10 o'clock?

2. $63 + 8 =$

3. $91 - 7 =$

4. $58 - 50 =$

5. $5 \times 4 =$

6. $34 + 4 =$

7. $1 + 6 + 2 =$

8. $78 - 9 =$

9. $35 + 0 =$

10. $69 + 20 =$

GENERAL REVIEW 14

Solve each problem mentally.

1. 18 + 0 =

2. 16 + 27 =

3. 45 + 9 =

4. 73 − 7 =

5. What time is 1 hour before 8 o'clock?

6. 8 × 3 =

7. 7 × 0 =

8. 78 − 16 =

9. 29 + 60 =

10. 93 − 8 =

GENERAL REVIEW 15

Solve each problem mentally.

1. 30 − 0 =

2. What time is 1 hour after 7 o'clock?

3. 76 + 15 =

4. 11 × 1 =

5. 38 + 60 =

6. 80 − 9 =

7. 97 − 10 =

8. 5 + 6 + 2 =

9. 29 + 8 =

10. 2 × 6 =

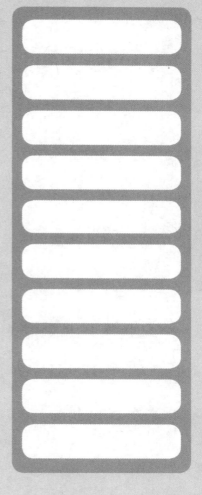

Notes

ANSWER KEY *Mental Math Level 1*

WEEK 1

1. 6
2. 2
3. 10
4. 5
5. 1
6. 9
7. 7
8. 3
9. 8
10. 4

WEEK 2

1. 9
2. 1
3. 7
4. 2
5. 5
6. 8
7. 10
8. 3
9. 4
10. 6

WEEK 3

1. 7
2. 9
3. 10
4. 8
5. 5
6. 10
7. 5
8. 7
9. 9
10. 8

WEEK 4

1. 5
2. 9
3. 9
4. 6
5. 8
6. 8
7. 10
8. 10
9. 7
10. 9

WEEK 5

1. 5
2. 10
3. 6
4. 8
5. 9
6. 6
7. 10
8. 9
9. 7
10. 10

WEEK 6

1. 9
2. 5
3. 8
4. 7
5. 5
6. 7
7. 9
8. 10
9. 8
10. 10

WEEK 7

1. 13
2. 10
3. 18
4. 12
5. 19
6. 11
7. 16
8. 17
9. 14
10. 20

WEEK 8

1. 20
2. 6
3. 8
4. 4
5. 12
6. 14
7. 10
8. 18
9. 40
10. 22

WEEK 9

1. 13
2. 13
3. 11
4. 13
5. 12
6. 14
7. 15
8. 11
9. 11
10. 15

WEEK 10

1. 21
2. 24
3. 32
4. 23
5. 20
6. 37
7. 22
8. 32
9. 21
10. 33

WEEK 11

1. 37
2. 34
3. 31
4. 35
5. 36
6. 31
7. 27
8. 34
9. 32
10. 32

WEEK 12

1. 24
2. 14
3. 27
4. 35
5. 16
6. 14
7. 23
8. 14
9. 33
10. 44

WEEK 13

1. 82
2. 65
3. 93
4. 81
5. 84
6. 48
7. 85
8. 103
9. 84
10. 90

WEEK 14

1. 27
2. 45
3. 97
4. 58
5. 31
6. 76
7. 62
8. 53
9. 87
10. 65

WEEK 15

1. 22
2. 44
3. 80
4. 61
5. 53
6. 74
7. 41
8. 86
9. 94
10. 67

WEEK 16

1. 56
2. 42
3. 82
4. 63
5. 35
6. 95
7. 45
8. 70
9. 63
10. 84

week 17

1. 43
2. 67
3. 93
4. 52
5. 47
6. 65
7. 37
8. 82
9. 72
10. 28

week 18

1. 93
2. 22
3. 81
4. 52
5. 85
6. 74
7. 31
8. 64
9. 36
10. 37

week 19

1. 94
2. 88
3. 89
4. 85
5. 88
6. 93
7. 72
8. 71
9. 91
10. 93

week 20

1. 8
2. 4
3. 9
4. 2
5. 32
6. 67
7. 43
8. 16
9. 29
10. 57

week 21

1. 4
2. 2
3. 8
4. 11
5. 37
6. 46
7. 85
8. 52
9. 28
10. 97

week 22

1. 5
2. 1
3. 4
4. 4
5. 3
6. 7
7. 3
8. 4
9. 1
10. 4

week 23

1. 12
2. 21
3. 47
4. 14
5. 32
6. 93
7. 56
8. 63
9. 80
10. 61

week 24

1. 59
2. 96
3. 21
4. 1
5. 4
6. 58
7. 46
8. 74
9. 52
10. 98

week 25

1. 6
2. 1
3. 5
4. 0
5. 7
6. 3
7. 8
8. 4
9. 9
10. 10

week 26

1. 8
2. 13
3. 20
4. 6
5. 14
6. 11
7. 7
8. 15
9. 17
10. 5

week 27

1. 4
2. 18
3. 27
4. 77
5. 36
6. 57
7. 16
8. 69
9. 59
10. 86

week 28

1. 12
2. 13
3. 10
4. 11
5. 13
6. 11
7. 16
8. 14
9. 13
10. 11

week 29

1. 16
2. 28
3. 29
4. 16
5. 7
6. 15
7. 29
8. 7
9. 12
10. 6

week 30

1. 27
2. 8
3. 16
4. 17
5. 27
6. 32
7. 4
8. 9
9. 34
10. 21

week 31

1. 72
2. 55
3. 24
4. 43
5. 31
6. 61
7. 15
8. 44
9. 43
10. 62

week 32

1. 48
2. 27
3. 56
4. 35
5. 16
6. 62
7. 76
8. 81
9. 44
10. 73

WEEK 33

1. 83
2. 42
3. 55
4. 37
5. 74
6. 59
7. 26
8. 7
9. 85
10. 18

WEEK 34

1. 16
2. 38
3. 86
4. 65
5. 9
6. 25
7. 49
8. 56
9. 89
10. 77

WEEK 35

1. 25
2. 11
3. 66
4. 19
5. 23
6. 34
7. 18
8. 39
9. 39
10. 17

WEEK 36

1. 61
2. 13
3. 28
4. 56
5. 82
6. 45
7. 31
8. 40
9. 33
10. 35

WEEK 37

1. 0
2. 0
3. 0
4. 0
5. 0
6. 0
7. 0
8. 0
9. 0
10. 0

WEEK 38

1. 2
2. 6
3. 5
4. 10
5. 7
6. 3
7. 1
8. 9
9. 8
10. 11

WEEK 39

1. 8
2. 20
3. 16
4. 10
5. 2
6. 12
7. 4
8. 14
9. 18
10. 24

WEEK 40

1. 9
2. 18
3. 27
4. 15
5. 3
6. 6
7. 21
8. 36
9. 30
10. 24

WEEK 41

1. 28
2. 40
3. 48
4. 12
5. 8
6. 20
7. 32
8. 36
9. 16
10. 4

WEEK 42

1. 6
2. 0
3. 5
4. 8
5. 24
6. 18
7. 30
8. 0
9. 1
10. 21

WEEK 43

1. 11 o'clock
2. 5 o'clock
3. 1 o'clock
4. 7 o'clock
5. 3 o'clock
6. 6 o'clock
7. 4 o'clock
8. 8 o'clock
9. 9 o'clock
10. 10 o'clock

WEEK 44

1. 7 o'clock
2. 9 o'clock
3. 12 o'clock
4. 3 o'clock
5. 10 o'clock
6. 8 o'clock
7. 2 o'clock
8. 6 o'clock
9. 11 o'clock
10. 5 o'clock

WEEK 45

1. 12
2. 14
3. 9
4. 31
5. 19
6. 12
7. 47
8. 36
9. 16
10. 34

WEEK 46

1. 57
2. 50
3. 18
4. 16
5. 58
6. 49
7. 69
8. 44
9. 13
10. 0

WEEK 47

1. 19
2. 71
3. 8
4. 52
5. 37
6. 88
7. 10
8. 39
9. 10 o'clock
10. 97

WEEK 48

1. 36
2. 83
3. 13
4. 18
5. 56
6. 32
7. 35
8. 63
9. 12
10. 41

WEEK 49

1. 83
2. 7
3. 10 o'clock
4. 18
5. 42
6. 93
7. 5 o'clock
8. 24
9. 50
10. 81

WEEK 50

1. 11 o'clock
2. 71
3. 84
4. 8
5. 20
6. 38
7. 9
8. 69
9. 35
10. 89

WEEK 51

1. 18
2. 43
3. 54
4. 66
5. 7 o'clock
6. 24
7. 0
8. 62
9. 89
10. 85

WEEK 52

1. 30
2. 8 o'clock
3. 91
4. 11
5. 98
6. 71
7. 87
8. 13
9. 37
10. 12